I0151448

Whores Are Always Melancholy

poems by

Jess Mize

Finishing Line Press
Georgetown, Kentucky

Whores Are Always Melancholy

ACKNOWLEDGMENTS

First appeared in *UnbrokenJournal*: The Ghost Who Walks, The Gaseous
Vertebrate, Cult of Suffering, Sick Muse
First appeared in *Harbinger Asylum*: French Translations of Chinese Poetry,
Sound of Death
First appeared *New Pop Lit*: A Night Like This and PBR
First appeared in *Poetry Quarterly*: Storm
First appeared in the AgitProp issue of *Sein und Werden*: Loire
First appeared in the zine *Anti-Heroin Chic*: Now I Know how Joan of Arc Felt
First appeared in *InkinThirds*: Flightless Birds

Publisher: Leah Maines

Editor: Christen Kincaid

Cover Art: Gabriela Barkho

Author Photo: Jess Mize

Cover Design: Elizabeth Maines McCleavy

Printed in the USA on acid-free paper.
Order online: www.finishinglinepress.com
also available on amazon.com

Author inquiries and mail orders:
Finishing Line Press
P. O. Box 1626
Georgetown, Kentucky 40324
U. S. A.

Table of Contents

For Libby and Sophia

The Ghost Who Walks

April through December, the months drag by; waiting for the slumbering season.

In May I celebrate Spring by gathering roses and lilies, crocuses and violets, hyacinths and narcissuses in lush meadows; until Pluto rises from his subterranean abyss and makes me his bride.

In June I practice the piano. Debussy and Scarlatti, mostly. I hear my parents scraping their balding heads, yesterday's lobster still beneath their fingernails, with the subtle pull of my Humbert Humbert spiderweb.

Vacation comes in July. You can find me naked on the beach, in sunlight without deception, staring at the cloudless sky, completely numb. At least my fair skin is becoming bronze by gold.

August already! The languorous heat stupefies me so I vegetate indoors, watching blasé classic movies in black and white. Nostalgic for garbage. Desperately in search of lost time.

September brings the hope of a slight respite. The colours of the dead leaves on the dirty ground are a small consolation prize; a reminder that all hallows eve is near.

I spend the whole of October preparing for the Day of the Dead. I become an ascetic. I meditate to the sound of laughing children; vandalous teenagers with two dozen cartons of eggs and hot sauce in their bags.

On November the first, I feel alive for the only day of the year. All the ignored dead souls console my loneliness. Like a real ghost I walk amidst them, passing out trinkets and listening to their problems. Some grab ahold of me tightly, gasping with short breaths, unable to speak even to say thank you. Others ask about my life. Imagine! So I take them on a walk through the forest glade, where I passed my misspent youth and learned to be like them; alone, pale, disconsolate. Most want me to deliver a message to their families, their friends. They should as well ask to put it in a bottle and drop it in the ocean, to be recovered in future centuries. No one listens to me either.

The Jazz Singer

Every few years I break myself down and start over in the dives and crannies of New York. My family's opinion and their reputation was heavy when I started off, leaving Georgia and singing all over the world. In Dubrovnik, Buenos Aires, Moscow... Opening in a jazz club I was too young to even be in. The rebel, the outsider, the solitary bird. I still put it away. Their approval or lack of. There was no need to carry their ideas with me. I cannot let that feeling in my body, I would not let that feeling go.

Alice

Did Alice see herself
backwards when
she stepped through
the looking glass;
and did she shut her eyes
when falling down the
Rabbit Hole
to Wonderland?

French translations of Chinese Poetry

What a magical day it would be to have one's first absinthe. Dreary Sunday like those of London. Rainy with overtones of auspicious morality. A steely atmosphere. Disgusted with the week we put our thoughts to more distant recollections. The insolvent future in liquescent folds of time. Oh the boredom of dissembling, futile repetition of the most dated of gestures. Turning now to an unusual ceremony, the schematics of which may entice some to a rather incipient loathing. This is expected and unless… For this, the melodic intonations of Scarlatti. Sun-flushed windows of morning. The fictional qualities. There is something soothing though about the words on the page. The absence of fixed colour panels.

Infatuation

Infatuation has its unique charms. Jealousy and privilege which lead to god-awful scenes that go unreported because of the incipient nature of their provocations. An action is performed because…there is always an intent which requires specific action. To grope, to laugh, to dance. Banish words and embrace sensation. This is the respectable mode of experience. Live longer, devour more bitterness. Gloom sweeps at the closing of every capitalist store. Everybody does it, don't say you're not the same.

A Night like This

night comes on like a cloaked poet,
strangely austere.
the moon rustles in its silver bag
bestowing ethereal light upon
groves, back roads,
and graveyards;
where young hearts
explore old pleasures anew.

this map is redrawn
with each generation,
cartographs of pleasures and purgatories,
these Baedekers catalogue every trifle
using binary code.

but under this sky and these stars,
iridescent white on midnight blue,
Rhianna's Swarovski crystals,

in this season of our youth and
of our put off despair,
ecstatic peace can spare
us an interlude.

The Gaseous Vertebrate

Cazart!...A dreary haze of gray falls across the afternoon of the city. The branches of thick-foliaged trees come to life with the motion of the wind. The surf three-hundred miles away breaks and crashes over rocks and piers and sends banana boats swaying. Rain is in the air along with a fresh, cool breeze.

It is five o'clock in Asheville and behind me from the radio it is Steely Dan...Oh no, Guadalajara won't do..."

In the spring and fall rain is exquisitely pleasant but in the summer it is altogether a gift from the gods. Soft drums of thunder; quick jagged bolts of lightning; incredibly white leaving the faint impression of yellow with a breeze that can give a mystic an orgasm.

Wind-blown hyacinths treat the senses to a honey-like essence. I keep expecting Peyton Loftis to come in seeking shelter from the approaching storm and leaning over my shoulder to be my muse, our cheeks imperceptibly touching. She has a bottle of La Famiglia and makes a couple of drinks, setting my glass by the typewriter. She sips hers and looks directly into my eyes with her half-closed brown eyes searching my every thought. I take a long drink from the old-fashioned glass as she walks over to the mirror and slowly undresses, admiring the curves of her body and allowing me to, as well. She flutters gracefully to again lean over my shoulder and to see what I'm cranking out this evening, and enchantingly whispers, "What'll it be, work or play?" laughing softly like a goddess.

On waking, it was time to close and it had yet to begin raining.

Storm

storming on an August afternoon. Jazz lightly playing: A Frank Sinatra moving picture on the television screen. Thunder and the leaves swaying dark green iridescent with the soothing rain resounding as if a waterfall in the North Carolina mountain ranges. It grows exceedingly dark as the metallic grey-blue sky transforms into a steel-grey monster. I have grown fond of this dreary weather, especially as it feels like the mystic stories of Edgar Allen Poe. A something altogether haunting and mysterious is a late summer stormy afternoon; the clandestine eyes of Ligeia. I have avoided solitude through fairy tales and like the sky today I have wept profusely when the bitter sun shines. Gilded sculptures and horrible romantic novels of the 19th century echo from the shallow depths of my past imagination. Pale lightning ignites amid the zephyrs like an angel intertwined, corresponding with the heavens and with earth.

Pleasures of the Sensory

Alluring evil of pale poisonous flowers,
Rhythmic chant of a sleepless dervish in ecstasy,
A melody by Scarlatti, inspiring our solitude;
Knowing, hearing, becoming, each,
I say a blessing for our lady of Urbino and collapse.

Loire

Loire: the current of the longest river. Imperial lights of the new century. The belongings of the nations. A claim to or for what is right. The miserable people. Exclamations of unhappiness not heard because of the greater goal explained. Everyone forgives and the youth of this culture relaxes in the tumult of love. Haze of emotions. Throngs of the future, disgruntled by and reluctant to condone the past that had created them. We all love someone, or we all love something, either way we are able to sleep through the night. Somehow we are able to forgive this love or forgive ourselves for feeling a certain way. The earth recalls all things. At least every action is processed. So with your individualism being expanded, the earth turning around as always; how did you expect to be free? Our planet is a captive too. Despairing over our sins, the earth is an ocean of tears somewhat condensed; salvation is but a concept, and the wicked have their thoughts too.

First Date

How are you?
Smiling and kissing her cheek,
softly, very close.

A winter night, immense fog
lingers from the overcast day.

As I pull away the nest of her hair
it glistens and seems natural on a
night without moonlight.

The air was scented sweet
like distant burning fruit
as we walked towards the car
on our first date.

I took lilacs in a two-liter coca-cola
to her front door.
And knocked.
And waited.
And smiled as I have said;

she wore a chilled white sweater
with a black skirt and white stockings.
Flowing hair and a cynical flicker
to her agate-coloured eyes.
She seemed much more striking than a Botticelli.

In the car we listened to NWA
and I smoked a cigarette
feeling the blind excitement of her presence.

I said: *you're beautiful.*
She said: *please let's not be silly,*
I know.

The Stars, the Bars, The Cars...

Long ago love was her eyes of topaz crystals and her smile of atavistic contempt. A pleasant combination of thoughts mingled with the sound of distant rhythms and the legendary rituals of the most native of barbarians. Evening settled over the villa with a certain air of something reoccurring. The cafés and squares were filled with unwanted romances and bitter desertions. From the summit at the edge of the cliff a young girl watches the explosions and hears the thousand thunders and the immense rising smoke beyond the mountains below and across the valley.

Sky

My sadness forms like
waves of the sea.
It undulates with the
tumult of passions
and flames of red lust
lick at my heartstrings.

Sunlight speckled on her
copper skin.
Bronze by gold.

Charity flashes
in a brief flicker of love.
It is the key.

And bad feelings
suddenly skirt away
like so many nimbus
clouds.

Cobalt blue sky like Ferreira.

Libby

everywhere.

I can see you in everything.
your veins are in the leaves.
the sunlight glimmers in your eyes, and
I catch glimpses of you in shadows.

The birds sing along with your voice,
they sing enchanted songs,
with your sweet words.

my love, you are everywhere
but,
nowhere to be found.

Paradoxical

Sloth rises up and forms in me like dew from the clouds in the morning. And alas, there is no sun to rejuvenate my blood. Pale and ineffectual. Like as if nothing ever changes. Sleep and wake. Repetition precedes itself. Would you say, my dream of 26 January last? Do so little that your sloth precedes you. One thinks one has a soul, therefore one has a soul. It is a result of the English language. Nonsense. Clarion call, perform thy duty. *In the fashion of many others, I shall place it aside.* I am too weak for madness. More decrepit than King Lear; the only energy I have is spent in sulking. Ephemeral consolation. Ah well, tomorrow and tomorrow and forever.

Kind of Blue

standing on the porch
looking up at the moon.
the clouds are so low
they look like
spun cotton;

I can almost touch them.
it is like you are
looking down.
only they cannot compare to those
wispy sparkling eyes of yours.

Cult of Suffering

Dropping out. Tuning out. Dreaming about a blonde-haired suicidal, surfer girl. A connection and a glimmer. The release of desire left you weak and unsatisfied. How to achieve a moral perspective? Pile on the sentimentality. Irregular stained glass. Elements of suspense and a closed perspective. The sunlight streamed through. The day was hot. The languid sun sparkled in the crystal waters. It takes forever. Cult of suffering. Golden laughter. I don't go outside any longer. My sadness comes in waves. It is almost soothing.

And Now I Know how Joan of Arc Felt

thoroughly depressed; wanting to die. Self-pity passes over me like a wave of mutilation. Wa-aa-avve. I have visions of nightmares over Joan of Arc. Hopes and dreams departed in an icon discarded. A pendant that did not make the life journey. Tears like snow globes. Inside their own fantastic little fake plastic world. Haven't I cried enough? In a thousand different ways. The answer is always no. There are more ways to suffer in heaven and on earth than are dreamt of in my philosophy. The wicked one. The being of light. The one who enjoys suffering. A hell of one's own invention.

Pabst Blue Ribbon on Ice

It is nice to know someone is happy. I could cry all night if the gods would let me. But it takes a lot of energy to sustain what may be termed a violent emotion. The real and the imaginary. Memories like recent events. Certain roads and deserted landscapes. A setting that stretches for miles. You cannot be this miserable forever. At some time, in the future, you will die with your collective thoughts, emotions, and imaginations. Neither they nor you will prolong existence. It is a circle badly drawn. To wit, the repetition is superficially concealed. Recriminations of what you do not have. What if one's body and one's mind and the actions they create are the projection of one's soul? If only science had not far surpassed my sloth.

Scot Fuckin' Free

mythical liquescent opal moonlight. Jesus take me forever from my despair. Tedious outlook of a Cimmerian landscape.

A question of, is it her? is it one's idea of her and that potential for yourself? All is silent with the suburbans as natural life swarms, germinates and dispels relentless energy streaming something more powerful than science. Oh my god. The world spins 'round always.

The love you crave cannot be purchased. To satisfy your desires you need an annotated trucker's atlas and a serious deficiency of remorse.

Sick Muse

She loved the bright vermillion flushings of the fresh blood. The pleasant release sent euphorics tingling along her nerve endings. Her hysteria subsided in warm, gentle waves as the blood streaked along her wrist and mingled with the very hot water of the bathtub. Metric was playing on her device on the edge of the sink. *Fantasies. I'm not suicidal, I just can't get out of bed.* These days she liked to listen to Metric or Lana Del Rey. Really nothing else did it for her any longer. She kept her left wrist submerged in the water, so the blood would not clot around her freedom. The hot water had become a peppermint mess, a *white blood cells* bath bomb dropped in and spreading around her naked body. She let out a deep breath, feeling the endorphins travel through her blood stream and spark up her heart like a sizzling telephone wire. She let her head slide back against the wall and closed her eyes. For a few seconds she could annihilate herself, her mind lucid, her exhausted body soaking and reveling in the scalding, soporific water.

Flightless Birds

She looked forward to the day of her funeral
As if it were her wedding,
And she was Grace Kelly.
But really she was the bride of death
And her longings for
The black embrace,
To lie down in darkness,
Bubbled over in the
Gleam of her eyes like shaken champagne
Bottles on New Year's.
An effervescent death vibe,
Mantra of dark malevolent birds
And rhythm of staccato'd heartbeats.

Hysterical fevers all of them. The slightest emotion betraying lusts, motives; even the subconscious of dreams

Lo-Lee-Ta

green sun perfume
virginity misused

for sale: my nymph
hair: blonde, lips: velvet
size 0 yet she's gained
affection

  autumn evenings; Tchaikovsky
on repeat
   faded blossoms, amber
Leaves, so discreet

stayed up to see the dawn
casting spells upon my lover
  treating the lithe angles
of her thighs like Joyland

honey for the stickiness;
her hand in mine was
sticky sweet like honey,
palms gelatinous

who is your idol, my little china doll?
all legs and arches
and lecherous thoughts.
still one of those pin-up models
like Cara Delevingne?

Sound of Death

Beautiful flowers line my path
to hell.
I stop to smell every single
one.
Patiently, I work my way to
the end.
Eternal damnation will smell
like gardenias.
Death will be a symphony.

E, Blanc...

Snowfall in January. More than I've ever seen. The whiteness invades everything in the picture. Beautiful, cold, enervating. Sometimes the only way to get by is to blot out the recollections of what once made you happy. Those memories have to not exist in order to move and toil, in this life.

Escape

An escape: from a place, from a life, from a conversation, from a landscape, from a colour, from an aroma, from a person, from a sight, from a collection of words in a certain order, from music, from laughter, from looks, from Ohio, from the past, from the present, from the future, from the crystal of her sea-green eyes, from her vicious sentimentality, the clever ironicism of her voice; from failure, from judgements, from considerations, from addiction, from fear, from boredom, from ennui, from strength, from weakness, from appearance, from the wars, from first meetings, from goodbyes, from hope, from loss: An escape.

Departure

Weeping willows with the confidence
of the wind hiss:
silence is our only bliss.
Nymphs pace on tips of toes,
eager to shower the golden sun-child.
Sky vast; air abrupt.
The breath of waves,
aromatic as a hyacinth in Cybele's hair,
strikes a remorseful chord.

The time to fall in love with has fled

Whores Are Always Melancholy

Sitting at the graveyard
Listening to the crickets
Looking at constellations.
The headstones and statuary relics
Bring with them a feeling of
Coming home.
Thunder in the distance knocks
Like an insistent tenement super
As rivulets of sweat
Roll down my forehead.
The breeze is salty and
The apple ale is sweet,
Like cinnamon.
A black and yellow monarch
Flutters gently across a
Wisp of my hair.
I love the purple haze cast
By the twilight.
There are no shadows,
Lightning flashes in the distance.
It is red, orange and blue;
Creeping thunder and salty air.
Smoking a cigarette,
Thinking of you.
Always you.
It will be like this when I am
Dead.
Then you will
Meet me at the cemetery gates.

Jess Mize was born in Spartanburg, South Carolina. She grew up in a rural area where she loved to ride horses and listen to her mother, Garland, read Stephen King stories. She began writing poetry at the age of seventeen when she first read the *Illuminations* of Arthur Rimbaud. At present, she spends her time taking care of her daughters, Sophia Pompeii and Libby Leagones, and composing poetry whenever the muse inspires her.

www.ingramcontent.com/pod-product-compliance
Lightning Source LLC
LaVergne TN
LVHW051613080426
835510LV00020B/3267